The excitement of a project like the *May Anthologies* springs from the proof it offers each year that literature is alive. The large crowd both of submissions and of people wanting to be involved in production point to the place that reading and writing still claim in our consciousness.

As with any collection of diverse writings, a look through the volumes reveals widely varying tones and voices. Does the cadence of this poem catch you up, speed your pulse? Or this story, does it make you feel your own clumsiness through the blunders of the characters? Whatever your reaction to a piece, whatever your suspicions of the writer's intentions, one thing is sure. Through choosing words as a form of expression, the writer has demonstrated a certain faith that language will affect you.

The *Anthologies* encourage students to exercise this faith and to take an active role in moulding literature. Many thanks to those who enable the project to continue – the Oxbridge colleges who provide the bulk of funding, the executive editors, the editorial staff, and Emma Horton, who has dealt with people and production with impressive efficiency and dedication. And thanks, of course, to all those who contributed.

Martha Kelly
Editor

GW00702712

The May Anthology
of Oxford and Cambridge Poetry 1997

Varsity/Cherwell

First published in 1997 by Varsity Publications Ltd and Cherwell (Oxford Student Publications Ltd).

This collection © Varsity Publications Ltd 1997. All rights reserved. No part of this publication may be reproduced, stored in a retrieval system or transmitted in any form or by any means – electronic or otherwise – unless the written permission of the Publisher has been given beforehand. Copyright on individual poems reverts to author on publication.

ISBN: 0 902240 22 6

A CIP catalogue record for this book is available from the British Library.

Typeset in Times and Garamond by Emma Horton
Printed and bound by Ennisfield Print and Design, Telfords Yard, 6-8 The Highway, Wapping, London E1 9BQ

Original concept: Peter Davies, Adrian Woolfson, Ron Dimant
Cover design: Michèle Kitto

Further copies of this book are available from good bookshops in Cambridge and Oxford.

Editor: Martha Kelly (Cambridge)

Executive Editor: Christopher Reid

Publisher: Emma Horton
Design: Michèle Kitto, Tim Harris
Typesetting: Emma Horton

Cambridge College Sponsors:
Clare, Corpus Christi, Downing, Emmanuel, Fitzwilliam,
Gonville and Caius, Jesus, Newnham, Pembroke, Queens',
Robinson and Trinity.

Thank you also to the Cambridge Editorial Committee, the
Oxford staff, and to the Oxford colleges for their assistance.

Contents

Introduction

It was not long after graduation, when I was still living in Oxford, that I bumped into one of my old tutors, in the covered market. He asked me what I was up to. I told him I had just finished writing a poem. He pounced at once. "Ah," he said, "I've met a poet! I must go home and tell my wife."

Why had I expected anything else? He must have remembered me as one of his dimmest students, sitting through classes in almost total silence, while sharper minds and quicker tongues were taking this or that genuine poet to pieces. Knocking the stuffing out of Coleridge. Feeding Ben Jonson through the mincer. That was the critical style of those days. I wonder if it's any different now.

There were students who wrote poems too, of course, and published their own magazines to put them in. I wrote my own share. But that was not quite the same thing as being a poet. A year or two after the encounter with my tutor, I was asked by a woman at a party what I did. "I'm a poet," I replied. Her free arm windmilling the air for balance, she fell back into a flower-bed. This was less, I feel, in the spirit of having seen Shelley plain, than of sheer amazement at my effrontery. It made me more

cautious in my subsequent self-introductions. "I'm a writer...
Oh, poems, as it happens."

Universities and university towns are probably not the kindest
places for aspiring poets, which is why I think the Oxford and
Cambridge undergraduates and postgraduates whose poems are
gathered here deserve particular congratulation and
encouragement. The air around them is so thick with erudition
and knowingness about poetry, that to engage in the reckless act
of writing a bit yourself demands not just the usual, hard-to-
come-by skills and qualities, but bravery as well. This anthology
celebrates the feat. If lectures had to be skipped, and essays
neglected, to get any of these poems finished, so much the better.
I hope that, when told, the tutors of 1997 were less sarcastic than
mine way back in '71.

Christopher Reid
1997

Homecoming
Nick Laird

From the word go the Ulster way was to leave.
And again a son's gone off. Gone across, gone south.
And got lost on the long cast. Gone posh. Gone soft.
But at vacations the reeling-in, the rolling home,
expecting banners, drums, feast-days in his name,
only to find the town unforgiving, furtive,
straddled by an Orange Arch – "Welcome here Brethren",
but not the place's native faithless children.

Learning gone to their heads, back-agains lob questions
like grenades at the dead, assess their own core and character,
talk of the light of Ulster in the evenings. Before retreating.
Emma and I used to throw sticks over the bridge into the river,
to see whose came out from the dark arch first. Easier
to go with that sinewy flow than bed down and raise a stir;
stay. An accent is at least a token vocal gesture,
a hook caught in river-roots while the line spools off elsewhere.

Think of an Irishman, whose boat's come in, sitting
at the airport. Well that's me. I'm the man in the joke.
The lynch-pin of the bobsleigh team, the one that won't begin
'til the track's been gritted. The simple harmless bloke.
But Irish were deceivers ever. Sharing water and air
with those who murder, and doctors, birthdays, names,
taints you. I once became Jesus because of Brummie innkeepers.
Travelling through England after the bombs in Birmingham;

1

my expansive Dad, Mum large with me, my sister just a toddler,
nowhere would take us in. No inn. The luck of the Irish
where an accent, beard and bulk spelt suspect, terrorist.
Fair enough. But tough enough too. They slept in the car.
Ripples spread outward and outward. And blood being thicker
than an acre of seawater, distrust has more to offer.
I'm scared about that. About what that might mean –
these thoughts of an endless homecoming,

to this over-anthologised province, this skundered hole,
where the gullible and the culpable are forever interchangeable,
along with the good, the bad and the holy, where stray
seagulls swoop low over Lough Erne and Lough Neagh,
watching fishermen, by passed-on legerdemain, conjure
something from nothing, lures from wool and feather,
fish from water, their eyes fat and dead from swallowed lies.
I've always been fingers and thumbs when it comes to tying flies,

blind at reading rivers, at floats and knots an amateur,
but I knew a man who was a master. He knew the sharp tap,
grew used to the strike. He is only ever pictured at the river.
Trees splitting light, the quiet pool lit like a Big Top,
grass ringside seats, and him, ringmaster with a flyrod whip,
in the swim of it, standing in the river's skin, the lash
and crack of line and slack eluding us. I almost gave it up
after learning, at Dee's in Kesh, how to wash and gut the fish.

But riverbeds are not easy left. Old baits sit and wait to hook
your boots. One last cast. That splash. Lost by looking back.
The evening Dad saw an otter or something similar up at Millars'
I caught an eel further along the bank. Hooked him coming home.
A returning one who'd managed to outswim the traps at Toome,
and who wriggled like he was being tickled when I cut him.
For hours after his tail was an epileptic tiller,
his torso a wavelength. Ultraviolet. Even the cats wouldn't try it.

And so I imagine the path of the lure as mine. The bale-arm click
as it snags on rock or weed, the line taut as tendon,
the reel-in delayed, the spoon snug 'til tug or flick
releases it. And then the spinner teasing and ascending.
But I remember how it's common for returning salmon
to leap onto the ground instead of up-stream. And to drown
stunned in that thick shared air. The other way of getting home,

of stepping in the same river, of lastly coming among your own.

Driving at Night
Gill Saxon

Between illuminated towns the dark roads lie
Mile after mile.
For guidance, only the white line and the cat's eye
Punctuate time and distance.

All travelling is guesswork.

Some of the major junctions have lights
And there are signs,
But these are difficult to read at speed, at night
And names can be misleading.

Choosing a destination will not guarantee arrival.

The road map and the scribbled sketches from a friend
Are folded shadows.
Stars give a better bearing, but do not light that next sharp bend,
The cliff edge, the black ice.

In the dark, a map is only paper.

Steering into a skid is like telling someone lies
For protection:
Whichever way you turn seems dangerous; and so you close your
                                                                    eyes,

Release the wheel
And let things slide.

Don't die lie don't lie die
don't die don't lie
Turn the

Choosing Shoes Blues
Gill Saxon

Life's too short for choosing shoes
I said
Life's too short for choosing shoes
Oh life's such a short hop
Don't spend it in the shoe shop
Oh life's too short for choosing shoes.

Life was made for making love
I said
Life was made for making love
And you'd better make some
Cos it's gonna take some
To get the world out of this hole
You'll need a sturdy kinda soul.

Making love don't need no shoes
I said
Making love don't need no shoes
Step off of the mean street
Strip down to your bare feet
And feel that grass between your toes
Baby feel that grass the way its grows.

Drop them shoes and walk away
I said
Drop them shoes and walk away
Leave them for some bum
Whose life is more humdrum
Who eats and sleeps and reads the news
Man that cat'll love them shoes.

Life's too short for choosing shoes
I said
Life's too short for choosing shoes
So step up and make a stand
Go barefoot throughout the land
Cos life's too short for choosing shoes
I said just too short for choosing shoes.

Notes for an Aubade
J S A Lowe

I don't know if you know me very well yet.
Perhaps you do. Perhaps you think you do.
I'm the kind of girl who sits up late after
everybody else has gone to bed, talking to
herself and sewing paper cranes to the end
of the window pull. The June bugs thwack
the damp screens, knock themselves silly
and fall down, paddling in the dirt. I stay up
after I am tired of waiting for perspective, for
truth to hold out a blessing, just like a baby
all limp with tiredness jerks awake after
every sleepy nod and tries to look alert. I
prick myself to stay awake, I don't want to
miss anything even when nothing's going
on, even when I've had enough of a good
thing I still want more. So does it make
sense now why at sunrise I cannot keep
my fingers from your skin, from circling
suggestively along your thighs? My eyes
close against my will, shut tight without
asking my permission. But I can still hear
the grey seagulls crying out to each other
through the intervening space, just as they
do every morning, just as the sea will come
right up to the old stone steps
even if I do fall asleep.

The Torso of a Goddess
J S A Lowe

The night before her surgery
she knocked on the doors of all her artist friends
until she found someone with time
and the ability to draw her nude

Back in her room she stripped to the waist
and quick fingers and sure eyes
brought out on cool paper appraisingly
what had been remarked so often with wonder before

Freedom lies in remembering without reliving
she reminded herself as she dozed off
prepared to wake in a few hours
and find a slightly lesser, no less perfect world.

Un Jour Sur la Plage
Abbie Carpenter

The bloodless carnage of
The streaming shoal of boats
Speared by their masts
Heaves rippling restless
With the licking nurture
Of the salty balm.
The cotton reel lighthouse
Set up for skittles
On the esplanade shades
The fisherman who walks on the water.
Stubbed toes
Skitter the splashed ink,
Seaweed black and
Rocky blue hue.
The white sun of the picnic plate
Sweats
Purple grape-juice.
A plum-stone beetle
Nuzzles the wine pool.
Sand on my paper
Spatters like a star,
And round and round
The sea sighs
Breaths of deep
Sleep.

Untitled
Sean Walsh

If you spent this long in the city rain; if you
Looked at everyone with a raincoat, and wondered
About the hairstyles and choices that people take.
Then you'd begin to feel a little lost; you might
Begin to lose yourself a little, and begin to cultivate
Roses, or an accent; you should try to forget it.

If the world of accumulating possibilities hit you
While you were staring in a newsagents
At pornography and chocolate; you might begin
To think yourself down with the lost, lucky and free;
Because there are no pagodas in your life
You don't own up to delight in the city.

You don't remember the long rides home, that
Singular who bent over a little too far one day;
Do you think you may have missed your love
Through shyness; no, you never knew her games
Or what those sunglasses meant, never really got
The sort of virtue she saw in afternoon sleeping;

So, the one who could have made you happy
Probably walked past you one day; and I thought
'Fine', or 'nice', or 'cute'. I lost what you lost,
And then the next moment I thought mostly
About a truck that splashed me dirty.
But the corridor of love didn't suddenly shut.

Do these things ever go away? Was there
A natural? Is this something like it?
An umbrella blooming will pull you again
Over towards a world which falls in place;
You catch the line which takes you direct
Home; you fold more potential today.

Photographs are Superficial but possible fantasy
Sean Walsh

Pushing the door to the attic left dust
On our hands, and hands in the dust.
Pulling up splintered fingers.
We fumbled, because there could be
Webs or rats or bats or stuff, or
We could fall through to the blue bathroom.

Up there, we found the black-gilt album
Of our father's life. This shot of him,
Dancing with Grace; offering Cary
A cigarette. Dad, your Mother (fixed smile),
And the unmistakeable, utterly trustworthy face
Of Jimmy Stewart. Next, the firm handshake
On the Presidential lawn (his cleanest cuffs ever),
And evening leaning towards Jackie
Year later mourning next to Bobby.
Then Frank, Sammy, Dino, Dad at the pool;
Oh ancient epitome of cool!

Or that's what I saw.
That's how it should be.
That's what I'll believe.

What'll you find, kids, when you break in?
The album of fantasies we're making,
The fur and patents, flaunting and perfect faking?

Well, we'll be again by your eye;
It's yours to glossily redream our life
If dead or dull at fifty, save us; try
To find a patina: make us something.

Fierce Substance:

A Collage for V
Adam Foulds

Nature hath meal and bran, contempt and grace.
Cymbeline

"at some point i would like to find out who or what the sun is"

The poppies in their sunlit trance
know, facing warm sugars to the sky,

and the nettle clump, hazy with venom,
brewing air to a numb stench,

and the wasp-grub, writhing in a gall,
fuelling its pulp with soft proteins.

*　　*　　*　　*　　*

Mild summer, and on polite lawns
sprinklers wave silver combs or waltz.

Mild summer, and I slouch in this empty house,
my mind, in your absence, turning prose

until I remember the occult pull of your blood,
my kisses at your throat,

or the warmth and slender resilience
of your ribs,

your heart vividly coming to
under my hand.

*   *   *   *   *

In that narrow bed, half uncovered,
one shoulder chilled and stiffened

as with the grey starch of clouds,
the other was a peaceable valley

where your breath grazed over my chest
and sleep-broken words flickered like swallows

over the wheat of your hair and
early light through the window hung

*   *   *   *   *

Coagulations of traffic. Boredom.
The machine hacking up tape after tape

we didn't want to hear. The sun
through the smeared windows

thickened to a revolting paste
soured with our cigarette smoke

(our fifth and sixth, respectively.)
Our route was obvious on the map:

a sprig of cartoon yellow,
but we had to wait.

The traffic wheezed together
like a dusty accordion,

reeking, going nowhere for ages,
and we had to wait.

*   *   *   *   *

Outside we drank and exchanged childhoods:
careful warning and welcome.

Late sunlight just catching
the wicks of the flowers,

I remembered following my father
round the gentle garden.

It seemed a dead weight, slumped in the shed,
until the bag was split with a stab of the trowel,

a puff of strange smoke,
and then the powder my father scooped

was livid and burned in my hand.
We walked up and down the vegetable patch

salting the earth for new growth
with fierce substance,

dried blood and dried bone.

Rainshine for Paul
Adam Foulds

We ran from the cafe into shining rain
to see the brightest rainbow we'd ever seen,
the wet valley stilled in its lovely glare.

All-symphonies-solving chord or score entire,
weightless alchemy turning a few trees blue,
the sky seen into, or seam in creation
showing through, stunning single formula
for all seeing
                    fainting out of sight, erased with cloud,
returning, as we did, to the common light.

We found the usual weather of talk and friends,
lit with smiles, waiting in the crowded cafe,
then drove the unhurried open miles
back to your house, our minds still stained with brilliance
like the spectrum immanent in a glass of water
that needs only angling into the light,
a careful tilt towards the sun, to shine out.

The Ice House
Simon Proctor

We found it at the back of the house
beyond the broken fence where
shadows from the garden trespass.

A smudged path leads us
there again this evening;
an earthen mound shouldering

the last of the day's warmth,
its entrance mouths a stone zero
to the cooler north.

Stooping to some instinct
we prod the dark with dumb hellos,
measuring the centuries within.

It replies only in vowels, stretched like shadows;
an older language, half buried,
emptied of accent, time and place.

But in it we hear those others
down by the lake stabbing coffins of ice to haul
back across fields simple with snow.

Is this why we bring friends here,
listening in abandoned temperature
for the glottal shift of meltwater?

The Sun Room
Simon Proctor

I loved its separateness,
the way the cat would settle there
to avoid the maroon
swerve of blazers on school mornings,
the flushing, toast-popping
imperatives of other rooms.

I loved its vagueness,
its lack of function
except as an overspill
for toys, mis-matched chairs
and relatives on birthdays
or after christenings.

Most of all I loved its lightness,
even in winter,
bottled gas blazing
as if, at any moment, the whole room would
rip its moorings and balloon upwards
out of sight.

But, with the last of us gone,
a re-weighting.
Two filing cabinets, gun-metal grey,
£40 apiece;
a desk, formica-topped,
rescued from the shed;
stapler, desk caddy,
two wire trays;
the calendar on the wall,
hoop-la'd with our visits.

And when we come
with our own children now
it surprises us,
across the hall from the lounge,
how we hesitate
on the threshold of its new privacy.

Winter Wheat
Dave Pritchard

Above the Grampians there's a range of clouds
like a legendary country: the view's so clear today
you can't tell where it ends. Burin-burr
of ice on moorland, crisp frozen earth –
the world mapped out in textures, so finely
you look for the watchmaker's mark –
cars on the distant motorways, and winter wheat
pricked out beneath the snow-fields.

You've stopped shivering now. It's hardly cold,
feels more like thawing. The skin hangs
like rain on your forehead; your blood
slows with each beat.
Not long to snowmelt. You can shelter here
just a little longer. You'll wait it out –

Full Immersion
Dave Pritchard

And ripples return across the silence
of a still pool where, dripping wet, face white,
you stand seized in a net of glancing light,
as if at the focus of the violence
you suddenly realised. Emptied and whole
and overbalanced. At a crux, an end;
plunged like a cleanly dropping stone to send
concentric shockwaves running in your soul.

Things were never so simple. There's no voice,
"With you I am well pleased". But quietly sense
the tightening of a glancing net of love
around your heart; the ever-meshing choice
searching itself. The widening imminence
and long demand of all, around, above.

Words for the Cat's Tongue
Greg Norminton

Bringing milk for the pussens, Leo Bloom
Thought to give your rough tongue sense:
Mrkgnao, you said. *Prr* and *Gurrhr!*
(This not in English but a sort
Of feline esperanto). You
Have sense to disregard our babel,
Blind to the mirror's bland imposture,
Trusting only the stench of life
And the death-wish of the mouse.
Yet androgynous Bloom, cuckold,
Man of the Future (Who Is A...)
Watched curious, kind, your sleek gloss,
His translations otiose
As his bath-blown lotus-flower.
Yours is a language far from ours,
Beyond the inarticulate heft
Of office machines sighing *sllt*
And drunken men in wakes or pubs
For whom words can be treacherous.
What stands in your way? Human speech,
Height of a tower?

                        No, you can jump us.

The Queen of Spades in the rain
Fiona Coward

Damp whisper,
So quiet it drowns everything.

There, rain used to slant off the bruised, cloud-sodden hills
Like a promise:
Cool, damp fingers uncertain of her face.

Here it merely falls,
Collecting banally in concrete puddles,
Flashing neon with borrowed life at night.

Where she used to be,
The touch of rain lit up the subtle colours of leached,
Bleached ochre-and-green landslides;
Add a marble sheen to the blood-sharp rock;
Hang heavy in the air
Like some overwhelming sea-scent.

Bones are where the trouble starts.
The chemical composition of their half-live structure
Absorbs calcium, strontium,
Anaemic green-grey-dirty-yellow
Oxygen isotopes
And heaving sea-grey scents,
And writes them through her
Like words in sickly-pink rock.

The Queen of Spades walks on a beach at night
Fiona Coward

She looks back
At the long stretch of indistinct,
Night-pale sand she has covered.

She looks ahead,
At the vast featurelessness she has yet to walk.

She is lonely.

She has walked too far to turn back,
And the cyclops buoys wink only for passing ships.
No one will follow to call her back.

She wants to go home,
But can think of no other home than this –
A stubborn body
And an unforgiving mind,
Framed by the varying black, white
Paleness of the beach at night.

The edge of the axe
Tony Williams

The edge of the axe that falls
On a man's wondering and prescribes
Is often trivial; no doubt a scholar
Could tell us that it should not cut

But the weight of the head –
Oh, that weight is so heavy,
Bearing the mass of the world
In its dull and compact form.

Where the edge may seem laughable,
Producing litanies, bloodshed,
Bones and heads of pigs in graves,
The head's weight is irresistible.

Every religion must have its holy places
Where the weight of the world concentrates
And reveals itself
And mine are all in you.

New
Triona Kennedy

Daytime tumbles out of night
In a hard thick rain of flame and cloud,
Fallout glistering our skin, piercing blisters

Making us to turn in pain,
Stiff moulds flourishing in cracked soil,
Half-sunk like the Pompeiian dead, eating air

Vent your lungs with a mute wet roar
Hardfrozen muscles itching warm,
Poised to seize faith, frost drawn from rock

In a gasp, the seizure, the first, reborn.

The Dentist
Joanna Penn

I lay back, trembling a little,
as he raised me to his level, and watched as
he leaned closer and closer.
I felt his hot breath
as I parted my lips at his command.
With no warning
he entered me with his tool,
the alien feel of it filled my senses,
vibration obliterating reason,
bordering on pain,
it probed deeper and deeper into me,
exploring every cleft and ridge
pushing me to my limit
I arched my back
and clenched my fists,
gasping, gagging,
repressing the screams.
Then, as suddenly as he came,
he withdrew
and smiled. It was all over.

Sums
Frances Parker

I

again awkward
abacus beads leave
the familiar

you-
shaped:

II

I think of a cathedral stone
on stone, each
stone a potential flaw,

and how below
that threat kissers
kiss the graves
and light candles.

New Year's Eve at Blufton
Frances Parker

Outside Savannah,
in an uneven town with a PigglyWiggly
and a saltwater river, palmetto-bound,

we gather, perhaps
to dig for signs
of seeds we planted
in an easier community.

You, like an oak
voluptuous,
shoring your surroundings;

and you, like an imported orchid
pampered in the greenhouse
of a trust-fund child;

and I, like Spanish moss
languid
until waves leap in the wind.

We affirm the corrupted branches of the low-country,
with covert unease test friendship,
affirm our suspicions that our roots define us
     and separate us.

The Zoology Museum
J M Tyree

Science as song of still life. Bones of
      a hundred tongueless birds stuffed glassy in
            the branches of sawdust trees.

We speak of: a wing. That shade of green. Somewhere,
      a phonograph records a certain modulation of sound.
            It's a repetitive musical phrase translated

into dusty electrical impulses. A quick brush of feathers
      plucked from the wind which makes you
            perfectly still, from the skies which you

perfect. And so – we know nothing
      which is not still – And so –
            We know nothing.

The Faculty of Divinity
J M Tyree

This hand is not a miracle,
>> says the Very Reverend Rowan –
>>>> musing, gowned, in the faculty

of Divinity. Nor is your trembling at the sound
>> of your lover's voice – nor this patch of sky
>>>> we are allowed to see. Or the peace

of warming winds that sunlight weaves
>> within the light-tongued leaves. If
>>>> leisure and the season of your pace

grace you with the sight, a leaf may
>> topple in the turning flow of falling air,
>>>> and if the sun conjoins its creases to

your drifting thoughts, you may sense
>> how the seed is sown in just this now
>>>> for you – you become aware of delicate

embroideries of light, soundless tapestries of wind
>> bursting audibly into the flame of red-veined leaves,
>>>> the endless webs of interfused visions which

form the fabric of these days – But this is not miraculous –
   unless the more miraculous, your being unaware
      of how it was arranged – I say arranged because

I know no other way to speak. For you become aware
   of such a fruitful, branching chaos cured
      of any need to say –

               Who caused it?

Biographies

Nick Laird (Cambridge)
was born within five miles of where he still lives, in County Tyrone, in December 1975, and came to Cambridge in October 1994. He wanted to be a writer when he grew up but, having an aversion to poverty, he has settled for a training contract with a city law firm and a ring in his eyebrow. Ultimately he would like to be a shaker and a mover.

Gill Saxon (Cambridge)
is a former newspaper journalist currently reading English at Lucy Cavendish College. Her work often involved lonely drives at night in search of unmarked village halls where Parish Councillors would spend three hours discussing a planning application for a front porch. She also hates choosing shoes.

J S A Lowe (Cambridge)
Born in Dallas in 1969, J S A Lowe is an affiliated student in English at Girton College. At Mount Holyoke College in Massachussetts, where she studied Philosophy, she was twice awarded university prizes from the Academy of American Poets, and won honourable mention in the 1995 Glascock Intercollegiate Competition. After graduating from Cambridge this June she hopes either to attend Boston University's creative writing program in the fall, or to run away to Mexico with her lover.

Abbie Carpenter (Oxford)
was born 25 May 1977 in London, one of three sisters and a brother. She moved to Cornwall in 1979; was educated at Truro High School; and is currently reading Classics at Hertford College.

Sean Walsh (Oxford)
was born in Leicester, 1973. He read English at Wadham College, then taught telephone engineers in Poland. He is now back at Wadham as a first year postgraduate student working on Dryden. He may leave the country again, since Blighty is going to the dogs. He likes poems and books and stuff.

Adam Foulds (Oxford)
was born in London in 1974, and is currently completing his degree at St Catherine's College. He has published poems and reviews in several journals. He intends to continue doing so from a new home in Athens next year.

Simon Proctor is at Trinity Hall, Cambridge.

Dave Pritchard is at King's College, Cambridge.

Greg Norminton (Oxford)
An English finalist at Regent's Park College, Greg has written a number of plays for stage, screen and radio. These include The Third Half (published by the Playwrights Publishing Company), Pedestrian (Grand Jury Special Prize, Fuji Film Scholarship 1996), Welter and Butterfly Voices (Oxygen 107.9 FM). Most of his poetry is actually prose that misses the right-hand margin.

Fiona Coward is at Trinity Hall, Cambridge.

Tony Williams is reading Philosophy at Queens' College, Cambridge.

Triona Kennedy (Cambridge)

is studying English Literature at Churchill College. She is into theatre and dressing up. As she's only twenty, she hasn't got two small daughters, and doesn't live in a charming cottage in Warwickshire.

Joanna Penn (Oxford)

is 22 and currently studying Theology at Mansfield College. Mansfield is a small but very friendly and active college and Joanna has tried to keep the masses entertained by holding the posts of JCR Social Secretary and RAG Representative. She enjoys being in the sun, going to the theatre and leaving England whenever possible! She is particularly passionate about Palestine, having worked there and travelled extensively in the year before university. She is an active member of Amnesty International and eventually hopes to work in international politics.

Frances Parker (Cambridge)

is a pseudonym, but if she did exist she would study History at St John's, and emphasise the fact that any obnoxious Americans you meet are not her: they are bound to be from the North.

J M Tyree (Cambridge)

Mr Tyree is the name that keeps appearing on my letters year after year. I am a pilgrim from ruined America, who spends his nights conversing with statues and his days recording birdsong. I am a theologian but despise all trades. I especially dislike writers. I wish I was a fish – a grouper, for example. I was born very early in the morning – for this, Mom, I am sorry